WHERE FAITH FLOWS

BY

Martha J. Griffin

La Tracambre, Inc.
Publisher since 2007

First Edition

Printed in the United States of America

ISBN 978-0-615-25687-0

I am so grateful for having the time, energy and thoughts to produce a second book of poetry. I attribute this accomplishment, of course, to Almighty God, family, friends and acquaintances. To those who have touched my life in both positive and negative ways, I thank you. The positive support has obvious results, but the rough moments have given me a greater incentive to think and grow outside of the box. God has truly been a mind regulator, providing enough good days and creating enough sunshine to make possibility a reality.

___Love

TABLE OF CONTENTS

*****

With God nothing

shall be impossible.

Luke 1:37

WALTZING

The body and mind, moving in sync,
Causes a rhythmic sensation that
Emits an invitation for all things
To sway in time to the silent song.

As the dance ripens, everything is
Persuaded to remain in the magic
Of the moment and be transformed
By the tranquility of the encounter.

GRATITUDE

God is so grateful when He sees
That we desire to do His will;
As He appreciates those bumble bees
Who provide honey nectar still.

God created beautiful nature trails,
That could not have grown on their own.
He created man, males and females,
To make his magnificence known.

God can do what none other can do;
Bestowing blessings when we pray.
His goodness permeates to renew;
Gently healing spirits everyday.

© 2001 Martha J. Griffin

DEPENDENCY

Things that you get addicted to
Only open pits that swallow you,
Up into a life that allows another
To take advantage and to smother.

Restraining you from natural talents;
Keeping your life off balance;
Convincing you it is the way;
Taking bad risks from day to day.

Conning people soon runs out
Once they see what you are about.
Family members struggle to cope.
Avoiding enabling is a tightrope.

The decision to stop is yours,
Perceiving choices it restores.
Freedom is possible to regain;
Casting old habits down the drain.

A spiritual life will provide a center;
A system with God as the mentor.
Building more strength each day
Learning as you watch and pray.

11-19-05 © Martha J. Griffin

Christmas

The Christmas season is here
Time to celebrate the birth
Of Jesus Christ our Savior
Beginning his time on earth.

Long ago people far and near
Came to see the miracle child.
There he lay in the manger,
Greeting them with a smile.

The three wise men brought gifts
After joyfully following the star
To the sacred place it led them.
No distance would've been too far.

The holiday is named for Christ;
A tribute for what he did for all.
He was ordained from the womb
To answer his father's call

November 20, 2004 © Martha Griffin

4

BOUNCE TO DUNK

Relying on the approval of another
Invites manipulations, for sure.
Pretending to care like a brother
They can offer bad for what's pure.

Left not only feeling deceived,
Because the words seemed so sincere,
You cope with those who believed
The con artist with all their gear.

Vivid memories try to fade
As months, then years go by.
Not allowing time to jade,
The mind rebounds to rectify.

Even the unconscious mind
Will finally be able to let go
Of the feelings left behind;
Erasing memories like a pro.

6-30-06 ©Martha Griffin

LINGERING ON

Years have passed since I've seen you
Yet memories keep coming through.
We've had a long time, it's true.
But a hundred years would be too few.

I miss your mischievous smile,
The magnetism that was not mild,
The conversation destined to beguile,
The ease of your personal style.

I remember you in the doorway,
Hesitating with what you had to say.
Although it was a bitter- sweet day,
Loving thoughts of you still stay.

© 2001 Martha J. Griffin

FORGIVENESS

To be forgiven is like a yearned gift,
Especially when we feel remorse.
It may not come as fast or swift
As we want sometimes, of course.

Reasons to be forgiven may be small
But, for ones you value, it's painful.
Wanting to be first to break the wall
Yet wondering if it will be gainful.

Unforgiveness creates a negative bond
That keeps both parties in slavery.
Forgiveness provides the magic wand
Releasing the hold, showing bravery.

Unforgiveness always saps our soul
Needed for peace of mind each day.
It also keeps our thoughts on hold
Until we let go for the better way.

10-1-07 © Martha J. Griffin

GROWING PAINS

I refuse to step back into oblivion
Back to days stuck in mire
Times when I was so confused
About what I was even to desire.

My ground has gotten more solid
As I trust in God to lead the way.
Depending on man is no answer
I would be left on my own anyway.

When I step out at the wrong time,
God steps in to pull me back
It's like he says, "you're not ready.
Wait until I provide the track".

He lays out the track gradually
Dependent on results of tests.
With much love he watches us
And lets us know his requests.

There are steps to everything
And preparation is ongoing.
Whenever there is progress,
You can feel yourself growing.

God has the atmosphere in mind.
The avenue he already mapped.
The plan carefully drawn out
To keep us from being trapped.

Man can talk a good game
But unless they are lead by God
They can cause much confusion
And make your life so very hard.

I don't claim to have the answers
To everyone's problems in life
I just know that I want to avoid
Unnecessary heartache and strife.

If it means standing alone awhile
Until a solid ground is revealed,
I must be content with this condition
Because I refuse to be unhealed.

1-10-07 © Martha Griffin

In Judgment

In evaluating a situation,
What is the consideration?
The amount of people is key.
How many should there be?

Time is a necessary fixed fact;
Eating and sleeping to subtract.
The problems to circumvent
And all the others to prevent.

How to discern what to pursue
When it is not clear what to do.
Stableness of mind to think
If troubles have you on the brink.

Judging by just observation
Avoids seeing any complication.
Refusing to look any deeper
Avoids needing a dust sweeper.

Easier to quickly turn away
And continue with the sway.
Rendering an awaited decision
Without even adequate vision.

7-27-06 © Martha J.Griffin

10

IT Doesn't Matter

It shouldn't matter what others think.
It's what we are striving to become
And what we think of ourselves
That counts as the rule of thumb.

Chances are others don't really know
What our heartfelt desires are
And what we wrestle with day to day.
Their opinions may come under par.

Too much uneven comparisons are made
Based on perception of a similar basis.
Too quick to see oranges as apples
Or to compare a desert with an oasis.

11-8-07 © Martha J. Griffin

JUDAS TOUCH

To everything there is a season
And to some there are no rules.
Such as attaining for selfish reason;
Desperate to think all are fools.

Judas betrayed Jesus with a kiss.
His legacy remains with us still.
A message we can't afford to miss
In order to stay in God's will.

We need to hold on steadfast
To what we know is right
God has kept us in the past
And we're always in his sight.

Sometimes we can be blind
When trickery is in the mix.
Evil creeps up from behind
Too sudden to think or nix.

3-11-05 © Martha Griffin

RUN FOR FUN

It's fun to be me, as in breaking free.
For when my life differs from yours,
I know that I need the strength to be
Steadfast in all types of downpours.

I can't be content trying to pretend
That I want to be what I'm simply not.
That I'm worth only the money I spend;
Running to catch up, all tied in a knot.

Living superficially, hidden by veils
And hoping to gain something implied.
When reality shows up and pretense fails
Feeling betrayed because I complied.

Loyalty can be a mixed bag of trust
For family, friends, colleagues and all.
However, to oneself, it is a great must
Because we need to heed the right call.

January 4, 2007 © Martha Griffin

TWINKLING

Twinkle, twinkle little star
Of Bethlehem so bright.
Shining from the sky afar;
What is your message tonight?

Is the sparkle an invitation;
A celestial bidding to obey,
Sent out to each nation;
Helping to point the way?

A babe wrapped with love
Is surrounded by hay.
He is blessed from above
To be awesome from that day.

November 21, 2004 © Martha Griffin

KITCHEN MEMORIES

Cornbread made from meal
With bacon pieces inside
Liver mush made to appeal
With potato salad a pride.

Okra with tomato sauce
Fried in an open pan
Collard greens are the boss
The food smell just began.

Of course chicken is a part
When we think of a spread
Dumpling boiling is an art
From flour that was spoon-fed.

Ham is glazed with fruit
Baked to a succulent look
Sweet potato pie sure to suit
Thanks to a Southern cook.

12-18-05 © Martha Griffin

Responsible Unity

The seven principles of Kwanzaa
Apply to the individual and group.
As we strive for unity at home,
In the community and the nation.

Each strong person is able to be
More responsible in things that
Benefit the world around us.
Creativity enhances these efforts.

Respect and appreciation for
Each other will produce a
Cooperative mindset that will
Void the crab in the barrel affect.

We need to define ourselves and
Understand our purpose in life.
Faith in God will allow him to
Provide and guide us to that end.

12-4-05 © Martha Griffin

LEAPING

It's not wise to jump before looking.
One must find out what to expect.
Like what's up or what's cooking?
After all, it's showing self- respect.

Seeming to have good intentions
While focusing on another thing
Is not what the announcer mentions
As the event in the center ring.

When words don't match the actions,
It raises a red flag to beware.
It's time to be leery of factions
That seem to have no soul to bare.

Once you've been sold into 'slavery',
By those who think only they deserve
And think of their actions as bravery,
You learn to be cautious and swerve.

1-10-07 © Martha Griffin

Easter Story

It seems life, virtue and purity
Are key elements of the Easter story.
Because of the king's insecurity,
Christ died, but arose in glory.

It's difficult to keep a spirit down
When God has willed it to live.
It will flourish and not be bound;
Having an open heart to forgive.

3-6-06 © Martha Griffin

RIDING THE WAVES

Still waters provide the backdrop
When the tides seem nonstop.
Holding on as each wave nears;
Staying at peace with no fears.

Maturation provides the experiences
As doubt repeats its appearances.
Determination grows to withstand;
Spilling onto horizons to expand.

Negativity is intended to delay
Progress, if only for one day.
But, sweet still waters cleanse
Improving vision through new lens.

Lending an ear for truth and love
Gives the soul wings like a dove.
It's natural to hearken to God's voice.
He created us. We have no choice.

October 7, 2004 © Martha J. Griffin

CHRISTMAS JOY

Christmas joy is what we expect
As we honor the sacred birth.
The Yuletide spirit is in the air
And felt throughout the earth.

People speak and sing of gladness
In knowing that Christ was born.
Sent to free us from our sin
That can prick like a holly thorn.

As we decorate and give gifts,
It is important to remember
That, Christ's love is the glow,
For this holiday in December.

11-13-05 © Martha Griffin

Don't Give Up

If you need help you can go to the Lord.
He will not tell anyone about you.
He loves you. He cares about you.
Don't give up.

Sometimes it looks like you can not
make it.
Don't worry. God knows all about it.
So, don't give up.

You can make it. Keep the faith.
Everything will be alright.
Always pray and don't give up.

Gary Byers

© 3-3-07

21

IF IT HAD NOT BEEN

There were many ancestors who
Were able to bear the strife
Of more difficult days, yet pursue
Their goals and manage a durable life.

We would not be here to complain
About how life is not easy enough.
As we watch the world get more insane,
The survival of all becomes more tough.

We have a privilege to think about
The struggles that already took place.
How much they wanted to just get out,
But, instead relied upon God's grace.

Lessons on endurance through anything
Can be learned from just knowing
The strategies used to survive the sting.
By those who stayed instead of going.

12/12/2007 © Martha J. Griffin

MANNER OF SPEAKING

Body language speaks best
As it tells the unspoken word.
Even for what is not expressed,
A gesture can say the unheard.

Each girlish giggle gives away
The soft flutter of the heart.
Trying to keep feelings at bay.
But what does that twinkle impart?

The way one sits tells a feeling.
Leaning forward shows concern.
Arms folded is also revealing,
Indicating a thought that is stern.

Body language is good to know.
A revelation of the hidden thought,
Presented like a picture show,
That appears without being sought.

© 2005 Martha J. Griffin

NOT THE ONE

Button pushing is for elevators,
Electronic devices and such.
Their reactions are predictable.
Others too dangerous to touch.

It is wise to choose with care.
Before picking to select.
Testing out fertile, safe soil
To plant things to deflect.

The ground may begin to harden
And not allow roots to spread.
Leaves begin to wither and fall
And there is a drought instead.

© 2005 Martha J. Griffin

OBJECTIVE OF SACRIFICE

Sometimes judgment is misplaced
In speaking of spiritual dedication.
Efforts are not to benefit persons
Nor even a certain organization.

Belonging to a group is to render
One's service for a ministry.
For all actions are to God's glory;
Desiring to sacrifice continuously.

Offerings are on a personal basis,
According to our own heart.
How much we reverence God
Leads us to search for our part.

God is coming for his church
And wants it spotless as can be.
We become purer when we give;
Releasing blessings and jubilee.

11-14-2007 © Martha J. Griffin

POISED

The pencil, already sharpened
Was handy for imprinting paper
With defined erasable symbols.

Therefore, having been idle,
It was summoned to respond
To a need for specific notation.

Submissive, as it was poised,
It reported for the easy job.
Like a dart, it lead the way.

Scanning the surface and
With predicted opportunity,
It carried out the request.

© 2001 Martha J. Griffin

Presentation

How I dress or wear my hair
Is what I deem suitable for me.
But, just to keep it fair,
I don't mind if you disagree.

Some opinions have no base,
Except for an empty assumption.
No factual data to embrace;
Nothing but unbridled gumption.

It's not the outside showing
That's valued the best.
It's the heart inside knowing
What matters in any test.

Martha J Griffin© 2002

RAMPS

Crossing the terrain towards destiny,
Through happiness and challenges.
Sleekly maneuvering narrow tunnels.
As a squirrel through a hollow log.

Appearing afresh on the landscape
To experience more intricate wonders.
Part of a plan envisioned long ago;
Piece of a tapestry almost completed.

Off-trails were temporary detours
Shaping virtue, craft and endurance.
A predestined full circle arrival
Sets the stage for what lies ahead.

© 2001 Martha J. Griffin

REALLY? OH, REALLY!

Spinning tales of woes of another.
Someone's sister, aunt or mother.
Slithering here and there like a fox;
Hoping to keep truth in a box.

Confusing the present with before.
Trying to establish a false core.
Negating strength already known.
Incessantly wanting frustration shown.

SELF-PROPELLED

I woke up in the middle of the night
To a voice streaming from the TV,
Exclaiming: " Encourage yourself."
This made an impression on me.

At first, I resented the comment
Because I had grown tired
Of maintaining my peace
And did not feel inspired.

But, experience has taught, such
Things happen for a good reason.
I had been awakened before
With revelation in due season.

This too, seemed to be a message,
Transcending time and space.
Determined to get me motivated
To again increase the pace.

SUPERSEDING

Basic psychology states that much stress
Does not allow one to think properly.
Basic medical advice is that much
Stress causes physical problems.

To expect something other than
That is to expect the supernatural.
God then ushers in interventions
During those times of great need.

There is no rescue quite like His.
His equipment is effective always.
In the game of life, whatever comes,
God's tools can be called into play.

©2005 Martha J. Griffin

TIS THE SEASON

Now is the time of year
To expect a lot of cheer
Jingle bells ringing in the new
And carolers singing on cue.

Some long for a snow ball.
It is late December, after all.
But, it has not snowed yet.
Only rain makes the grass wet.

It had been warm for awhile;
Almost winter, yet so mild.
Temperatures are now colder
Caution for youth and older.

Winter clothing is being worn
And Christmas lights adorn.
We can do without the snow,
Just allow high spirits to flow.

©December, 2001 Martha J. Griffin

TROUBLE FREE

Memories of trouble, I use
When problems arise again.
Reminders not to refuse
Sources helpful back then.

Troubles are learning tools
Along life's merry way.
They can be the fuels
That make determination stay.

Strength is drawn from trouble
But, God will not overdo it.
Our faith in Him will double
As we forge on through it.

It seems He made the rainbow
To symbolize hope "anyway".
A guidepost for us to know
Victory can follow a rainy day.

TWO WAY

Most streets allow two way driving
Each side adhering to it allotted space.
Veering can cause certain disaster
If moving cars meet face to face.

Communication, however, is different.
It's necessary for two way interactions.
Alleviating anticipated misunderstanding
Through effective verbal reactions.

Assuming a correct knowledge,
With no input from the one in the know,
Is a careless act of trampling
Where no wo/man is privileged to go.

©2004 Martha J. Griffin

VISIONS

When do you stop doing the same thing
That causes more distress than benefit.
That delays development by a haltering hold
And blocks implementation of new visions?

Innovation is a breath of fresh air
That infuses new life into a stale situation.
If there is a stagnation in participation,
That is a signal that change is needed.

A little flicker can teach something new
That will quicken one's step and spirit;
Causing a pondering of how much better it
Would be to allow a mind to stay open.

©2004 Martha J. Griffin

WHEN

When I am feeling quite sublime;
When I'm having a trying time;
When I am simply floating in air;
When I experience some despair
I try to remember the feeling
That has truly been revealing.
I am able to determine the way
To spend each precious day.

No matter whose path I cross,
Or who has a comment to toss.
No matter if the sun shines
Or the phone has busy lines.
A negative can yield a plus
Without creating a big fuss.
Draw a line through it midway,
Signifying time out to pray.

12-31-04 © Martha J. Griffin

Thank you, God

I am grateful for your presence.
A place of refuge when the world
Has gone mad over what is
Presented as an alluring need.

The outward appearance is still
An unnecessary trap for those
Who are seeking fulfillment.
Ripe for the elusive picking.

Thank you for peace that defies
All understanding and the
Wisdom to know that, when it
Is God-given, man is bewildered.

Your answers to serenity prayers
Put things in proper prospective.
In the end, glory will be yours
As each knot becomes undone.

11-18-05 © Martha J. Griffin

BEHIND THE SCENES

The puppeteer works behind the scene;
Not out front, not even behind a screen.
Such condition can always be serene;
Difficult to analyze what can't be seen.

The puppets dangle and seem spastic;
Sometimes moving as stiff as plastic;
At times agile and supple like elastic;
Each time the performance is fantastic.

The only one who feels every tug
Is the puppet, who is guided to shrug,
By one who also makes it a jitterbug;
Then shifting the gear for a big bear hug.

The puppeteer is the only one who knows
What is really going on in all the shows
The audience can't see the highs and lows
Only through the puppeteer action flows.

10-8-06 © Martha Griffin

FORGING AHEAD

Passing through the thick and thin
Trying to master like a heavyweight.
Dodging perceived pitfalls to win;
Holding back forces that intimidate.

Persistent on keeping our ways
While being watchful and aware.
Locking in each value that pays
As we consider all that we dare.

Holding on for life's long ride
Swiftly or slow can be the trip.
Over hills and curves with pride
Sliding to base with a tight grip.

Looking back throughout the years.
Visions of events that have led
To the next horizon that appears
To create the possibilities ahead.

© 2001 Martha J. Griffin

HEARTH

It's the smile on the inside
That makes you feel so complete.
Where peaceful thoughts abide,
Buoying you off your feet.

Not dependent on circumstances
Beyond your ability to control;
Unaffected by mean words or glances
When you haven't bothered a soul.

When life presents hurdles to jump,
You can run on with that internal glow.
Each obstacle seen as a tiny stump
Allows bountiful blessings to flow.

Victories come large and small,
Personalized and tailored just for you.
Awareness is not known to all
A stoked hearth will carry you through.

LIKE THE WIND

I go fast on the treadmill;
Almost quick as the wind.
It requires a lot of will,
But losing weight I intend.

I started out with goal one
And ended up with more.
It became a source of fun
And satisfying to the core.

I stretch out with my might
As oxygen is breathed in.
My feet seem ever so light
As they quicken for a win.

Exercise helps my mind;
Keeping me calm and alert.
Peaceful thoughts I find
Abound, even as I exert.

© 2001 Martha J. Griffin

CONSISTENTLY TRUE

Truth is consistently deep
Not tangled in webs of deceit
Even if woken from long sleep
Out would come the same repeat.

Even after each difficult test
No confusion could be assessed
No changes with each inquest.
Truth yields yet another conquest.

7-27-06 © Martha Griffin

EXCUSE YOU, PLEASE

When one is talking to another
And a bit of off-base is spoken,
It can seem like two trains
Passing in the very cold night.

Some comments are said so fast
Before opportunity to respond.
Leaving behind only confusion
From misguided conversation.

It seems that at those times
The Holy Spirit gives advice
To move away and give space
To prevent fruitless conflict.

People tend to believe what they
Want to believe "to spice it up".
That's exactly why it is a favorite
Tactic of those planning evil deeds.

It is why God said don't fight it.
Leave the hard battles to Him.
They are unworthy and senseless;
LET GO. Let God be the avenger.

11-14-2007 © Martha J. Griffin

DRIFTING

Like a boat drifting off to sea
You drift away from me
Seemingly lost in time and space
I pray to God for more grace.

Refusing to believe the condition
Regretting each recognition;
Sleeping longer on recent days;
Watching for changes in ways.

Behaviors have gotten worse
Seeming like it is a curse.
Strength is needed to endure
Difficult days ahead for sure.

While Away

I keep busy with the necessities
Waiting for my energy to be refilled.
Grasping for help in my efforts
To keep all on an even keel.

The minutes, hours and days slip by
All without a single warning.
It seems that I spin around
And am still on the same dime.

What I need is a distraction
To get me off the merry-go-round
Perhaps something that I put down
But need very much to embrace now.

9-10-05 © Martha Griffin

Considering

If you feel you have each ingredient
That makes life easy and expedient,
You should run on and be obedient,
Resisting behaviors that are deviant.

To whom much is given, much is expected.
Your going further is what will be respected.
Mocking less fortunate ones detected
Negatively impacts your image reflected.

2-7-06 © Martha Griffin

WITH IT

Not complaining....just explaining
What should have been obvious to all.
Peaceful sharing...Not comparing;
Examining a card from a deck so tall.

Not complaining...Just explaining
That something human was overlooked.
Much assuming....Clouds still looming;
Of course, my schedule is overbooked.

Not complaining...Just explaining
That deceit appears in any disguise.
Much blaming....Many darts aiming
Relying on the One who is all-wise.

12-31-04 © Martha J. Griffin

Trinity Celebration

During this time of year we
Plan a Christmas celebration.
Grateful for belonging to Christ
We acknowledge our dedication.

Praise and worship is done
With the Word, dance and song.
Since we are celebrating God,
Peace and joy will come along.

We have a conscience because
The Holy Spirit dwells within.
It reminds us to do God's will
And helps us know what is sin.

Keeping Christ in Christmas
Also naturally fill us with
The type of Christmas spirit,
Lasting beyond the twenty-fifth.

©11-13-05 Martha J. Griffin

∞∞

MAY YOU BE BLESSED

∞∞

ABOUT THE AUTHOR

Martha J. Griffin has been writing poetry since 1997. Her themes seem to center around spirituality, self fulfillment and social issues. She has amassed experiences in a variety of arenas that have provided deep insight into the joys and pains of life. Martha is a founding member of the Grounded Voices Writers Group and has poetry in several publications. She is a social worker with two grown children.